Thoughts on tl

Religion, By a Deist

To Which Are Added, a Few Ideas on Miraculous

Conversion, and Religion in General

By a Theophilanthropist

Anonymous

Alpha Editions

This edition published in 2023

ISBN : 9789357943758

Design and Setting By
Alpha Editions
www.alphaedis.com
Email - info@alphaedis.com

Contents

THOUGHTS ON THE CHRISTIAN RELIGION
BY A DEIST

Religion, in some form or other, seems to have been observed by mankind, in all ages and all parts of the world; and considered as the most noble employment, of the most divine nature, and producing the most beneficial effects to society, of all the objects that ever engaged their attention: although from casual circumstances, and interested motives of individuals, there are as many modes and varieties of worship, as languages or nations on the face of the earth.

Europeans have in general embraced Christianity, as contained in the Bible, which *they* call the Word of God, as the only true and infallible system on earth, and which only can lead us to eternal happiness. This Bible, we have been taught to believe, is holy, just, perfect, and superior to the human understanding; so sacred, that to doubt or disbelieve it, would entail on us inevitable never-ending misery. This doctrine, being instilled into children by their nurses, and enforced by terror at a riper age, has long been assented to by the *generality of people*, who seldom think or enquire for themselves, but are always more or less the dupes of designing men.

But the times are now changing; the privilege of reasoning and believing for ourselves begins to be exercised—freedom of enquiry abounds; and the natural inherent right of speaking and acting according to the dictates of our own conscience (without injuring society) is happily enjoyed. Consequently, impositions of every kind, superstitious prejudices, and the long worshipped fabrics of civil and religious tyranny, are daily growing into contempt, and in all probability will soon be torn from their foundations, and consigned to that infamous oblivion which they so highly merit.

To come more immediately to the point—the Christian religion, as generally practised, presents itself as one of those monuments of ignorance and credulity, which the wisdom of the present generation is probably destined to overthrow, and to substitute a system more simple, more pure, and more agreeable to the dictates of reason. The Bible, upon examination, we shall find deficient in many of the virtues that have been ascribed to it. As a human composition, its merits have been greatly over-rated: it is exceeded in sentiment, invention, style, and every other literary qualification. The obscurity, incredibility, and obscenity, so conspicuous in many parts of it, would justly condemn the works of a modern writer. It contains a mixture of inconsistency and contradiction; to call which the *word of God*, is the highest pitch of extravagance: it is to attribute to the Deity that which any person of common sense would blush to confess himself the author of.

How are the rights and dignity of human nature insulted, degraded, and trampled upon! how are mankind blinded, deceived, and led away by this system! how is the honour and character of the Almighty affronted by the absurd and impious doctrines it contains! How is the sacred name of God abused and prostituted to the vilest and most execrable purposes, by his pretended worshippers! And all for one simple, evident end, to gratify the pride and avarice of unprincipled, designing men!

But something more than declamation is necessary to support these assertions. I shall therefore give the reasons why I disbelieve the Christian system, and all the arguments advanced in its favour.

As to the existing proofs of the divine authority of the Bible, whether internal or external, whether the evidence we feel in our own minds on examining it, or the miracles which are said to have attended its propagation, they are of no avail in convincing us of its divine origin: and I do not think, that independent of the prejudices of education, and the power of eloquence, there ever was a reasonable thinking man, who felt a sufficient internal evidence to convince him of the reality of the whole of its doctrines.

With respect to the public proofs exhibited by its founders, we find them no stronger than those in favour of Mahometanism, or perhaps any other system. Mahomet is said to have wrought as many miracles, preached as good doctrine, converted ten times as many followers, and was far more successful in all his enterprizes, however bold or difficult, than Jesus Christ. The Christians say, the Mahometan miracles were nothing but impostures; and the Mahometans say, with as much authority, that the Christian miracles were the same.

If the gospel system was so clear, so reasonable, and so powerful, as its advocates assert, what necessity could there have been for miracles to support it? If it had any foundation in reason and nature, there would have been no occasion for mystery, miracle, or revelation, to confirm it. A doctrine that is reasonable and true, will appear so to every unprejudiced mind, without the aid of any thing supernatural. Consequently, that system which requires miraculous assistance to establish it, and cannot be proved by human means, is neither reasonable nor true.

Supposing the Bible to have been written by divine inspiration, at the times, and by the persons mentioned in it, still it is next to impossible, that it could have been transmitted down to the present time pure and uncontaminated, even if there had been but one nation and one language upon earth. The variety of translations and editions it has passed through in the course of near 1800 years, if it has existed so long, (which I am inclined to disbelieve of many parts) and the continual improvements and alterations in human language, during that period, amount to a presumptive proof that the sense has been unavoidably mistaken, or wilfully perverted. A confirmation of this remark is open to all: let any one take the trouble of comparing different copies of the Bible, printed in the last and present centuries, or even in the same year, and he will often find a striking disagreement.

Admitting that the Bible contains the only doctrine by which we can obtain salvation and everlasting life, which of the numberless professions that have sprung out of it are we to embrace? One sect tells us that there is no salvation out of the pale of their church. Another tells us, that unless we believe and practise their doctrines, we shall surely be damned. Let us believe, therefore, in whatever particular profession we may, we shall be damned according to the principles of the others.

How gracious and beneficent is the Christian system! so perfect and pure that it creates so many different, distinct, and opposite denominations of believers; all of them right, infallibly right, in their own opinions, and proving their doctrine by the clear, in-contestible authority of divine revelation!

Many, as an excuse for countenancing a doctrine which they confess may not be true, say, that if the Christian religion be false, it is still very hurtful to attempt to overturn it; as we have no better guide, and no other method to restrain the passions and regulate the conduct of mankind; as it is the most perfect and beneficial system that could be devised. To determine this, we must look at its effects.

That doctrine which has the greatest tendency to secure our present and future happiness is the best; it proves itself to be so. That the Christian system does not tend to make us happier, may easily be shewn, by tracing its natural operations on the human mind. By it we are led to believe, that we are all miserable and ruined wretches; corrupt and exceedingly wicked from our very birth; naturally sinful, and opposed to the will of God in all our actions, words, and thoughts; and so far from deserving the common blessings of life, that if justice had been done us, we should long since have been cast into endless punishment. Tribulation, distress, and sore trials, are the common lot of mankind, especially the good. "Whom the Lord loveth he chasteneth." This world, it tells us, is a wretched, tiresome, and accursed place; a mere sink of guilt and misery; and all its enjoyments vanity and vexation of spirit. Though by the bye, those who are called sincere and pious Christians seem to be as desirous of continuing in it, and tasting the good thing's it affords, as the most sensual and worldly-minded sinner. It likewise instils into its followers such a servile fear, and dread of the wrath of heaven, that they can neither lie down at night, nor rise in the morning, without first attempting, by intreaty, flattery, and fair promises, to appease the Divine anger, and persuade the Almighty to permit them to exist in peace. Every accident is a judgement, and a prelude to further punishment. Every misfortune that happens to their neighbours is a warning to them; and they are liable every moment to be cut off by an avenging God, and sent to Hell.

While on the one hand, they represent the Deity as their servant, to assist them on every occasion, averting every ill they bring upon themselves, and extricating them from every difficulty and distress they plunge themselves into; on the other he is supposed to be a fierce, revengeful tyrant, delighting in cruelty, punishing his creatures for the very sins which he causes them to commit; and creating numberless millions of immortal souls, that could never have offended him, for the express purpose of tormenting them to all eternity. Thus they are generally miserable through life, in meditating on death and its supposed consequences.

The authority of the Bible appears still more doubtful from the absurdities and contradictions it contains; contradictions which all the sophistical ingenuity of reverend divines, with their literal meaning of this text, and spiritual interpretation of that, can never explain or reconcile.

In the very first chapter of the whole volume, containing an account of the creation, we find an inexplicable difficulty. In Genesis i. 27, 28, we are told, that "God created man, *male and female*, blessed *them*, and said unto *them&c*". But in ii. 20, we find that "there was not an help meet for Adam:" therefore, ver. 18, "God said, it is not good that man should be alone." And, ver. 22, "he made a woman, and brought her unto the man."

The Almighty, according to many parts of the Bible, is a perfect, unchangeable being. In Isaiah, he is said to declare, that he is "not as a man, that he should repent." But in other places we read of his repenting very frequently. He repented that he had made man. Having determined to destroy the Israelites, and having slain seventy thousand of them, "he repented of the evil," and spared the rest. He told Hezekiah that "he should surely die, and not live," but immediately repented, and gave him fifteen years longer. Jonah prophesied, in his name, that in forty days Nineveh should be overthrown; but the people believing him (though he did not perform his promise) and forsaking their sins, he "repented of the evil that he said he would do unto them, and did it not."

In one place it says, "Our God is a consuming fire;" and in another, "God is love." He is said to be Jealous, revengeful, and angry with the wicked every day; and pleased again as often as they repent: possessing all the good and evil qualities of man, that unstable, wicked, miserable, and insignificant worm. Notwithstanding all this, he is perfectly just, wise, immutable, and can never repent.

The Christian system, I venture to affirm, has been the cause of more evil in the world, than any other that ever appeared in it. By inculcating a belief that the Deity was a terrible God, an inexorable judge, taking vengeance on all his enemies; its professors, wishing to conform as much as possible to the character and disposition of *their God*, have in all ages acted with the same spirit, and upon the same principles:

"O let this strong, unerring hand,

Thy bolts for ever throw;

And deal damnation round the land,

On each I judge thy foe."

Inspired with the most vindictive hatred to all who do not subscribe to the principles they profess (who are, according to their faith, enemies; for they say, there is no medium or neutrality, "all who are not for us are against us;)" they have never failed, in any country, and at all times, when they had the power, to exercise the most cruel and detestable spirit that ever disgraced human nature. Not contented with insulting, oppressing, enslaving, and butchering the poor heretics here, but most humanely and charitably condemning them to everlasting torments hereafter.

During the first 320 years of its existence, Christianity occasioned the destruction of many millions of mankind. In the first part of this period, the Christians were the greatest sufferers; but in the year 312 Maxentius and his army of 200,000, were most of them drowned in the Tiber, or slain by Constantine, the Christian emperor; who, in three great battles, in one of which 100,000 were killed, reduced and put to death Licinus, the deputy emperor of the East; persecuted the Heathens and destroyed their idols, the symbols of their divinities.

In the twelfth and subsequent centuries, millions of Waldenses and Protestants were murdered in the south of France. How many millions lost their lives in the mad crusades for the recovery of the Holy Land! In Germany and Flanders, in England, Scotland, and Ireland, in South America. But I stop, or "I could a tale unfold, whose lightest word would harrow up the soul," chill the blood with horror, and draw forth curses from the grave against the very name of a religion which has been made the pretext for such cruelties.

Indeed, it is impossible to calculate the mischief that has attended the Christian system since its commencement. But, say its advocates, all this was done by Antichrist, or the false church. Which then is the true church? Not that which persecutes. And what church is that? The church of Rome? No: for that, after long struggles, no sooner became established in power, than it persecuted its dissenting sons with all the zeal and barbarity that it had experienced from its enemies. The church of England? No: for although that separated from the church of Rome, and rejected many of the errors and corruptions which had crept into it; yet no sooner was it fully established in Great Britain, than it very carefully trod over the steps of the mother church, persecuted Roman Catholics, and all Dissenters. The Puritans, who fled to this country for the sake of freedom of conscience and religious liberty, were no sooner settled, than they discovered the same illiberal persecuting spirit which drove them hither, and persecuted the Quakers in their turn; becoming as corrupt as any of the former churches. Each of them, while they were weak and defenceless, suffered by the murderous hand of its oppressors; and, when become strong and powerful, persecuted and martyred its feebler enemies. And I believe there is not a church in Christendom but would, if it could not convert, most gladly destroy all its opposers; had it that one essential and only necessary quality, *power*. For they affirm, that the world, with all its blessings, are nothing but temptations to draw them away from their true interest; and that unbelievers of every kind are their natural implacable enemies.

The carnal mind, say they, is enmity to God and his people, (themselves) and is in continual opposition to every thing good and heavenly; they must then of necessity wage an eternal war against all who do not acknowledge their system, as the only sure, guide to heaven.

The powerful blow which has been aimed at this system of faith by Paine's Age of Reason, has created a general and well-founded alarm. That work, to every bigotted or interested follower of Christianity, appears in a dreadful light indeed, as it is a direct attack upon their favourite, their dearly-beloved system of gospel faith, which exalts them, in their own opinions, so much above the rest of mankind.

The Christian theology is so favourable to the pride and vanity of man, that the slightest attempt to overturn it occasions an universal panic in its supporters, who immediately display all the ensigns of their cause, the pompous, high-sounding anathemas of Scripture, to frighten the bold invader of their aërial territories. So far they act consistently; for where they have no weapons or defence from nature and reason, fear and hope, though unfounded and delusive, are the only expedients left. By representing the terrors of their law in the most horrid colours, the wretched victim of their designs cries out in the depth of despair, "Lord, what shall I do to be saved?" The work is then in a certain way of success; the convert gives himself up to the direction of the church in all things, and is ever after the passive tool of its power. These converts are seldom or never made by pure reason and sound argument, for these would never answer the purpose; but the passions, which may be driven by every gale that blows, the fickle and inconstant passions, are so influenced by the power of false eloquence in violent declamations and vehement harangues, that the calm, even voice of reason is not heard, or is disregarded, amidst the bustle of jarring emotions; and the poor frightened wretch catches hold of the first object that is held out to save him from his fancied perishing and undone condition. Without ever once considering whether the profession they embrace is founded in nature and reason, they confide wholly in the piety of their spiritual teacher, leave their faith and hope altogether in his hands, and trust entirely upon his promises and power. Their belief he can alter or abolish at pleasure; for what he preaches they must adhere to; what he allows they must profess; what he approves must be true.

In fact, the Christian system has never yet been weighed in the impartial balance of reason, or received a candid trial in the thinking world. Force, fraud, and other unfair means have always been necessarily employed for its establishment. Had it been founded on truth, or consistent with common sense, its advocates would never have refused to submit it to reason, and the cool, dispassionate judgement of mankind. But they well knew that it could never stand the test, and this would be the certain means of its destruction. They therefore boldly and presumptuously tell the world, that it is beyond the reach of human reason, which is not competent to judge rightly of it. They confess that we cannot comprehend a great part of it; but at the same time command us to believe it, though we cannot understand it.

It has been the peculiarly honourable lot of Thomas Paine, the firm advocate of truth, the undaunted champion of reason, and the resolute and unconquerable enemy of tyranny, bigotry, and prejudice, to open the door to free and impartial enquiry. He has boldly entered the field himself, and taught the world, that no true system of principles, however sacred they may be held in the public opinion, and however strongly protected and enforced by the terrors of man's vengeance here, and eternal punishment hereafter, is too awful to be canvassed by reason, or too sublime to be comprehended by common sense.

The Christian system, as it is not consistent with reason, is declared to be above it; and should be received even if it does not appear clear and intelligible to our human capacities.

This by prohibiting enquiry, effectually prevents detection of falsehood and confirmation of truth. The doctrine is received upon trust, upon the credit of our forefathers; because, they taught, or rather said so, we must implicitly believe so, all the remonstrances of reason and experience to the contrary notwithstanding.

This is certainly a very great absurdity. For there once was a beginning to every system or theory in being; and at that beginning it was necessary to exercise reason as the unerring guide to direct in the choice or rejection thereof. If mankind were not only allowed, but necessitated to weigh every doctrine in the infallible balance of reason, at any time, why are we not entitled to the same privilege at present? Is our reason degenerated? Are our faculties impaired? Or rather, are we not far more wise and enlightened than mankind were centuries ago, and much more competent to understand and judge of things than they were? By the practice before mentioned, by that tyranny over the minds of men, which has ever been exercised in despotic states, the grossest falsehoods have been forced upon the world for realities, and the most detestable impositions established and maintained in all the strength and vigour of immutable truth.

But these arts, how long soever they may prosper, and by whatever authority they may be supported; though they may call to their aid all the powers of superstition and prejudices of education, and be assisted by the pride and deceit of hypocritical bigots and mercenary tyrants; still must they finally fall, and sink into contemptuous oblivion. The present state of society seems peculiarly adapted to the advancement of truth, and destruction of error. The sun of reason has begun to appear, dispelling the thick and almost impenetrable mists of ignorance and superstition, illuminating the most secret recesses of the mind, and will continue to increase in splendour, till it shine forth in one clear, unclouded, and eternal day.

The writings of modern philosophers have served greatly to illuminate the minds of the present generation. I will here, quote Pope's beautiful description of that *sublime and heavenly* religion, which mankind in a state of nature professed, contrasted with that distorted, gloomy religion which has been imposed on mankind by power and fraud.

> *"Man, like his Maker, saw that all was right,*
>
> *To virtue, in the paths of pleasure, trod,*
>
> *And own'd a father when he own'd a God.*
>
> *Love all the faith, and all th' allegiance then;*
>
> *For Nature knew no light divine in men,*
>
> *No ill could fear in God; and understood*
>
> *A sov'reign being but a sov'reign good."*
>
> *"Superstition taught the tyrant awe,*
>
> *Then shar'd the tyranny, then lent it aid,*
>
> *And Gods of conq'rors, slaves of subjects made:*
>
> *She, 'midst the lightning's blaze and thunder's sound,*
>
> *When rock'd the mountains, and when groan'd the ground,*
>
> *She taught the weak to bend, the proud to pray,*

To pow'r unseen, and mightier far than they:

She, from the rending earth and bursting skies,

Saw Gods descend and fiends infernal rise:

Here fix'd the dreadful, there the blest abodes;

Fear made her devils, and weak hope her gods;

Gods partial, changeful, passionate, unjust,

Whose attributes were rage, revenge, or lust;

Such as the souls of cowards might conceive,

And, form'd like tyrants, tyrants would believe.

Zeal, then, not charity, became the guide,

And hell was built on spite, and heav'n on pride.

Then sacred seeneth ethereal vault no more;

Altars grew marble then, and reek'd with gore:

Then first the Flamen tasted living food;

Next his grim idol smear'd with human blood;

With heav'n's own thunders shook the world below;

And play'd the god an engine on his foe."

From an attentive perusal of such liberal, enlightened writers as Pope, Locke, Hume, &c. who were not interested in forcing any unnatural systems upon mankind, whose only aim was the happiness of the human race, and from my own reflections, I have adopted the following *creed*, which I here submit to the impartial consideration of my fellow-citizens of all denominations.

1. I believe in one God, or first cause, wise, powerful, and good; and too far above the influence of human actions to be affected by any thing that can be done on earth.

2. I believe in the equality of men by nature (though so different by accident) the universal power of conscience, and the unerring authority of natural reason.

3. I believe the whole duty of man is comprised in this one great republican principle—Do just as you would be done unto.—My reasons for believing thus are, in the first place, that this first 'cause is wise and powerful beyond our conception, is clearly evinced in the wonderful formation and disposition of nature, exhibited in every thing that we have any perception of. That he is

good, the whole creation proves: for we find nothing made but what is useful, beneficial, and conducive to the happiness of the whole. And that he is too far above the reach of human actions to be affected by any thing that can be done on earth, is inferred from nature, reason, and experience: for the only idea that we can form of the Deity is, that he is a perfect, unchangeable being; and if we suppose that he so particularly notices the conduct of mankind as to be differently affected by their different actions, we must allow that he is an imperfect, changeable being, liable to be pleased or vexed at the mere will and pleasure of his creatures, and dependent upon the whim and caprice of *man.*

In the second place, it appears from the experience of mankind in all ages, that Nature, in the creation of man, acts impartially and equally; but leaves his talents, disposition, &c. to be regulated by mere accidental circumstances. That conscience has an universal power, is evident from the dislike and abhorrence, with which all mankind look upon actions that tend to the injury of society. And not to believe in the unerring authority of natural reason, would be to accuse the Deity of injustice for not creating us capable of distinguishing good from evil, and then punishing us for the evil we commit.

In the third place, that the whole duty of man is comprised in this one great republican principle, "Do as you would be done unto," has appeared so notorious to the world in all ages, that it has been universally agreed upon, as the unerring rule of action, and the basis of happiness: by the observing of which there can be neither oppression, deceit, or injustice of any kind. The duty of man is his interest; his interest is to make himself happy; and the surest and best way of doing this is to promote the prosperity of the whole.

Finally, that system of religion which contradicts itself, cannot be wholly true.—That which is not consistent with reason, or agreeable to the order of nature, must be false, as different from the will of the Deity, displayed in all his works:—And, that which tends to promote discord, pride, and deceit, is prejudicial to society, and ought to be discountenanced and opposed by every good man.

ON MIRACULOUS CONVERSIONS.

It appears to be the general opinion among the learned, that all matter is, more or less, in a continual state of transmutation; that there is a perpetual repulsion and attraction in nature. It is also the opinion of many philosophers, that the human mind is never quite stationary.

That locality, early habits, examples, affections, and associations have the greatest effect in forming the characters and opinions of men, is evident to our senses; and that after the character may be considered to be formed, a contrary course of habits, &c. of equally long or longer continuance will generally produce a contrary character.

Every attentive observer must perceive, that we sometimes dislike and entertain an unfavourable opinion of what we at another time approve and cordially agree to. To a cursory examiner these alterations may appear to take place arbitrarily: but to one acquainted with the philosophy of the human mind, accustomed minutely to trace the different links and associations which bias our ideas, they will appear, so far from being arbitrary or supernatural, to be perfectly natural and agreeable to the wise order of things. It would seem that most parties agree to the reasons given by the learned for such alterations, &c., except they be in matters of religion; here each party abandons the usual methods of philosophising, and has recourse to the supernatural interference of divine agency.

That extraordinary instances of conversion from vice to virtue, from error to truth, sometimes take place, for which the most profound and subtle reasoners fail to give satisfactory causes, is most readily granted; but still it may be said, that our not being able to trace a natural cause is no proof of there being none; for past experience has abundantly proved to the world the folly of such kind of inferences. Many things in science and philosophy are now even demonstrable, that formerly were, with equally good reason, considered to be miraculous or supernatural.

There are many reasons for considering the religious conversions not supernatural. There are no human criteria to determine when they are from God and when they are not. So many and so frequent impositions and deceptions take place, that there is no distinguishing the false from the true.

These enlightenments are equally claimed by every sect, however different in opinion. Now, supposing them to be from God, we are under the necessity of believing that there can be only one sect which can really have them; for it would be absurd to suppose the Immutable Creator of all things would inspire his creatures to believe, as true, opposite and different doctrines; and the confining of the divine influence to one sect only, certainly appears to be partial and arbitrary, and contrary to the saying, that "God is no respecter of persons."

People professing to be converted can never give a satisfactory explanation of their state, either to others or themselves, so as to do away all apprehension that they may not be actuated by impulse, fear, affections, &c., with a variety of other natural causes which every day make astonishing alterations in the minds of men.

We sometimes meet with individuals who at one time considered themselves to be inspired, and shewed every outward sign, and afterwards declare they conceive they never were.

Sudden and extraordinary changes frequently take place for the worse; but these are never accounted as supernatural. It appears that conversions most frequently take place after some circumstances which naturally have a tendency to fix the attention, soften the affections, affect the passions, and subdue the will; such as attending religious discourses, the deathbed of a friend, extreme pain, poverty, and distress, &c. Now, may not these be said to account for the first natural link? Then why should the rest of the chain be miraculous? If these observations were untrue, we might expect to find conversions occur as frequently among one sort of society as among another; but that is not the case.

It is observable in religious as well as in other operations of the mind, that those alterations which are the most sudden and vehement, are generally more transient than those which take place more gradually and after accountable associations.

We might naturally expect that those divinely inspired would be superior to the weaknesses of passion and imperfections of nature incidental to others; but our converts appear not to be. These supernatural affections are unattended with any discernibly supernatural effects; the possessors of them never perform miracles!

From these observations it is presumed, that there is abundant reason for apprehending that those conversions termed supernatural are nothing more than nature acting upon the mind of man, agreeably to those wise and immutable laws laid down by the adorable Maker of all things; and the reason of our terming them miraculous is, because we are unable with our weak faculties to trace the wonderful concatenations, and view the infinite variety of shades of which the intellectual part of man is susceptible. At the same time it is confessed, that it being a matter of internal feeling, and what cannot perhaps be demonstrated either way, no arguments on the subject can be hoped of any material benefit, either to the person who supposes himself to have it, but cannot explain it, or to him that has it not, and cannot conceive it.

Bristol,

THEOPHILANTHROPIST.

Feb. 18,1819.

A FEW IDEAS ON THE CHRISTIAN RELIGION.

It appears, that at least 99 persons in 100 take their religious opinions from their parents, and according to education, &c. without ever afterwards examining for themselves. Now, as this belief arises from causes that are variable and quite independent of the believers, it follows, that there is no security whatever for its being true, the chance being always against it: consequently, such persons' opinions are of no weight in the dispute.

A due attention to this consideration will, it is presumed, render the number of real believers and unbelievers in Christian countries much less unequal than at first we may be inclined to suppose.

The evidence for Christianity is founded on probabilities by a process of reasoning, not being intuitive or self-evident. The contrary of its being true can easily be conceived and does not imply a contradiction.

Owing to the different constitutions of the human mind, there always is, more or less, a certain difference of opinion upon all subjects in proportion to their want of self-evident proof. Then, when a subject confessedly has it not, ought we to expect from it those universal results which it could only produce by having it?

That there should be many who are not satisfied with the evidence of the Christian religion is not to be wondered at, since it is not of that nature to produce universal acquiescence. Where then can be the propriety of inveighing so bitterly against some for rejecting what, according to the nature of things, all cannot be expected to receive? Assuredly, the sin of doubting must be proportional to the evidence; then why should we attach the same punishment for disbelieving things that are not self-evident as we do for things that are?

With regard to the assertions, that "'tis their pride prevents their belief, that they make a Deity of their reason, and put themselves in opposition to Heaven," &c. it may be seriously asked, Are these assertors sincere in what they say, or is it merely spleen they, or any one, for an instant conceive it to be possible for a man in his senses, who has any idea of his Maker, or of himself, and is so deeply interested in the subject, to act in such a way?

There may be some reason for considering that doctrine to be false which might cause us to think existence a curse, rather than a blessing, and to entertain views inconsistent with the Divine Nature.

If the orthodox opinions be correct, how few among professors really profess! How small a proportion of mankind profess at all! It follows, according to even probability, that the number of the saved will be extremely small in proportion to that which is lost. Then, when a child is born, according to the laws of chances, there are very great odds against its being saved. Query, Whether it be a blessing to be born, to run any risk at all of endless misery, even were they very contrary of what they appear to be, greatly in favour of everlasting bliss?

Bristol,

THEOPHILANTHROPIST.

Feb. 18,1810.

DEISM EXAMINED

By A Christian

It has often been said, that if Christianity is not competent to withstand the test of reason, it ought to fall.

To this opinion I willingly subscribe; and so confident am I of our succeeding against our adversaries, the Deists, that I am for truly putting Christianity to this trial. That is, I would that there should be allowed as perfectly free discussion in all theological matters, that the "Age of Reason," and other works of a similar nature, should be allowed to be published. Let the enemies of our religion bring forward their objections as fast as they like; have we not, or our part, a ready refutation for every one of them?

The Deists, I know, have strongly contended, that many actions recorded in the Bible, said to have been done by the express command of God, are shocking to humanity, and in contradiction to all our ideas of moral justice. Such as putting whole nations to the sword; sparing neither age nor infancy; utterly destroying men, women, and children; leaving not a soul to breathe, &c. &c. But does not the Bishop of Llandaff reconcile this seeming incongruity, and vindicate the morality of the sacred writings by explaining, that, as the Almighty constantly superintends all the actions of nature, and in so doing permits, or rather causes smiling infants so to be swallowed up by earthquakes, or destroyed by other natural means; it is evident that these shocking transactions (as they are called) recorded in the Bible, do not militate in the least against the character of the Deity. The unbelievers certainly may bring a puerile argument against this profound assertion of the Bishop's; but the Christian who truly appreciates the real value of an unwavering *faith*, will have for such argument a thorough contempt, even before he reads it. They may tell us, if they choose, that nature being actuated by general and unvarying laws, it is not to be supposed the Almighty, in order to save a human creature, will perform a miracle. Or (to state the case more particularly) if a society of human beings will be so unthinking and imprudent, as to make their residence at the bottom of Mount Vesuvius, or Etna, that the Creator will partially suspend the laws of nature, in order that the burning lavas may not overwhelm them in destruction; or, that if mortals will be so presumptuous as to build their dwellings on the site of former desolations, as Lisbon for instance, that the Almighty will interpose, in order to prevent the recurrence of another earthquake; or that God will in any case partially suspend the eternal laws of the universe, in order to preserve a mortal that may be accidentally liable to be destroyed by their effects. They may tell us all this if they choose, and likewise, that this is quite another thing, to an express command from God himself to one set of human beings to annihilate another.—Thus we refute it all: such arguments are built on *human reason*, which it behoves every pious Christian to distrust!

Let them assert, that Jesus Christ himself, (if there was such a person) has proved the delusion he laboured under, since he actually and distinctly predicted, in more places than one, that his second coming would be in the days of the last surviving apostles, and that the apostles themselves sufficiently shew by their writings, that such was their opinion. Let them descant upon the description of his coming in the clouds (as related in the gospel) with the trumpets sounding before him, and call it a mere representation of human pageantry, and unworthy of being imputed to the Almighty Creator, who has millions of millions of worlds at his command! We thus refute the first part of this misrepresentation. Jesus, after predicting the destruction of Jerusalem, as we find it now related, speaks of his second coming, and gives a description how he will appear in the clouds, with the angels sounding their trumpets before him, &c. &c. and then continues thus: "Verily I say unto you, *this generation shall not pass away, till all these things be fulfilled.*" Now it is evident, that this last verse can only allude to the destruction of Jerusalem, and that the passage is misplaced by many sentences. It is true, we have no vouchers for this, nor can we perceive what instance there could have been for any one to have made the alteration; but as more than seventeen centuries have revolved since the death of Christ, and no second coming yet taken place, we are fully justified in maintaining the passage to be misplaced.

The Deists accuse us of all along suppressing their works, and certainly, in this respect, I must acknowledge we have acted unfairly. They say that most of the ancient productions on their side the question are lost; while the answers to them are still extant. From this circumstance they infer, designing and superstitious monks and priests, in order to remove every thing out of the way that might militate against their doctrine, destroyed all the writings of their opponents, while they carefully preserved those of their own party. It is likewise affirmed, the book entitled the Age of Reason, is a more formidable enemy to Christianity than any work ever before published, and threatens, should it become popular, to shake its flimsy fabric (for thus they speak of our religion) to its very foundation; that the charge of blasphemy is brought against it to suppress it, solely from fear of this consequence, and that our oft repeated assertion, "if Christianity cannot withstand the test of reason it ought to fall," is a mere mockery, for, in fact, we fully prove our intention is, never to bring our doctrine to such a tribunal. I am very sorry that this last charge against us is not altogether unfounded. Why should not the arguments of our opponents be allowed to be published? their authors would very soon, I am fully persuaded, meet with a total discomfiture, and find our Polemics more than competent to justify their own cause.

Every one knows that Mr. Paine was illiterate, that is, he only knew his own language perfectly, and had a smattering of French. Now, have we not bishops, deacons, lecturers, curates, &c. who are acquainted with Hebrew, Greek, Syriac, Arabic, Latin, and several other tongues, living as well as dead; and surely, it would be strange, if, with all this various learning, aided by their laborious researches into the antiquated writings of the primitive Christians, (those credible attesters of *miracles and witchcraft,*) that they should not be able to overturn such a paltry antagonist as Thomas Paine; who, alas! made use of no other weapon but *human reason*; who ridiculed *Faith* as a mere *chimera*; and maintained, that a strict observance of *moral virtue* constituted the only worship that was in *reality* pleasing to the Deity. Physiologists have asserted, I know, that the human brain is only capable of a certain degree of active energy, and that every additional talent we may acquire must be gained at the expence of all the other powers; and that, consequently, he who is familiar with a variety of languages cannot possibly think very profoundly in any, the whole of his intellect being absorbed, and the pure ideal part of it absolutely extinguished, in the complicated matter of grammatical construction, and the endless labour of committing to memory the various characters and innumerable quantity of words necessary for obtaining such knowledge. On the other hand, it is boldly averred, that he who knows his own language perfectly, and no other, may become, as it were, in his very essence, a compound of thought and reflection, capable of drawing, from the luminous stores of his own understanding alone, arguments that shall put to flight all the scholastic quibbling of the mere Christian linguist, causing the gloom engendered by his subtilties to vanish like mist before the sun.

The Deists accuse us of disturbing the last moments of the virtuous, and terrifying their imaginations with the prospect of eternal damnation. They say, that when such infatuated persons (whose bodily weakness renders them more than childish) become overwhelmed with the dreadful picture, and give way to the weakness of humanity, that we then infer, they had a proper sense of the enormity of their guilt before they died; and that we then exclaim, in the gloomy pomposity of the fanatic Young,

> *"Men may live fools, but fools they cannot die!"*

This quotation, when applied to the case in question, the Deists maintain to be unjust, and are for making a new reading, as being rather more applicable, viz.

> *"Men may live wisely, but fools they often die!"*

"Shame!" the Deists cry, "forbear to disturb the departing moralist with your strange dogmas! His sole trust is in his Creator, therefore let his last hours be spent in peace! Your interference is useless, and as it adds to the sufferings of expiring humanity, may well be termed impious and cruel. And further, what conviction can be gained from making public the imbecile and terror-extorted confessions made by the dying; for as Rousseau rightly observes, it is 'our reason that determines our belief, and when, through sickness, that faintly becomes impaired, what dependence can be placed on any opinion we may then adopt?'" All this seems at the first glance very striking and imposing, but is easily refuted. I shall confine myself, however, to only answering the latter part of the above. I maintain, then, that even shouting our dogmas in the ears of the dying,1 and thereby disturbing their last moments, is a mere trifle, when put in competition with the eternal advantages that may by this means accrue to their souls. It is well known, that Christians formerly, more generally than at present, did not scruple to compel men to become converts; and when the heretics, as they were termed, obstinately held out, they actually burnt them for *the love of Christ!* This manner of proceeding Dr. Paley has, in some measure, justified, 2 by affirming, that as the salvation of the soul is a matter of infinitely more importance than the well-being of the body, so these *converters*, who actually believed salvation to exclusively depend on the reception of their dogmas, may be said to be in some sort excusable, for endeavouring by all the means within their power to save a man's soul, though his body, in consequence, might be devoted to the flames.

1 Vide Life of M. de Voltaire.

2 Vide Haley's Evidences of Christianity, Part III. Chap. vii.

Some, I know, would go further, and urge, that even the burning of those who *were* converted by the threats of the holy fathers, was not impolitic, since it may be justified as the above principle, of preferring the welfare of the soul to that of the body. For might not a new-made convert, made so against the evidence of his own reason, recant, and thus render all the pious zeal of those *soul-preservers* quite abortive? Nothing more likely, and therefore to make sure of his eternal felicity, they were equally excusable in committing him to the flames. A similar principle influenced the pious Monk towards the unfortunate Jew, as related in a well-known but somewhat ancient story, concluding with these lines:

"Drag, drag me out—I freeze—I die."

"Your peace, my friend, is made on high;

Full absolution here I give;

Saint Peter will your soul receive:

Wash'd clean from sin, and duly shriven,

New converts always go to heaven;

No hour for death so fit as this;

Thus, thus I launch you into bliss!"

So said—the Father in a trice

His convert launch'd beneath the ice.

But enough of this bringing forward accusations and objections of the Deists, and answering them myself. Let them be brought against us in the regular way, and we will readily refute them. In fact, there will be some novelty in such an occupation to many of our divines, who have passed many years in the continued sameness of preaching to congregations who are much too passive and obedient ever to dissent a single syllable from the doctrine laid down. It is now several years since our Doctors of Divinity really exerted their talents, viz. ever since the first publicacation of the Age of Reason. I think it downright inconsistency for our authorities to prosecute those who publish works of this kind, seeing those works absolutely benefit Christianity. For did not the above production give rise to innumerable answers, each of which was sufficient in itself, to prove the divine origin and infalibillity of the sacred Scriptures! Read Bishop Watson's Apology for the Bible, for instance, a work *replete with genius*; a work which will confer lasting honour on its reverend author; and wherein we cannot perceive the *least traces* of what our adversaries term *priestcraft*, and not a *single sentence* which may be called *a quibble*. Another answer to the Age of Reason, by a *wit*, named Robert Thompson, also deserves to be made honourable mention of, as being neither *scurrilous nor contemptible*; as does likewise an answer, by a layman of the name of Padman, a work of vast *profundity*, and in which there is not to be found any *perversion or pitiful misrepresentation of passages* in Mr. Paine's book. Should these two last gentlemen be still in existence, and chance to peruse this, they will be extremely grateful, I am sure, for my thus noticing them; but they may reserve all thanks, for the encomiums I have passed upon them are nothing more than their real deserts. 1 But to conclude. Seeing, I say, that deistical works are beneficial to our holy and only true religion, by making its ministers exert their talents, let them be printed and freely circulated, and in so doing we shall no longer lay under the vile odium of being oppressors and persecutors for righteousness sake.

A firm Believer in the only true God, and a future state of Retribution.

London,

Jan. 30, 1819.

1 *There is also a Mr. S. Thompson, a member of the sect*

called "Free Thinking Christians," who in a work entitled
"Evidences of Revealed Religion on a new Plan," has
attempted to answer some of the objections of Mr. Paine; but
as his arguments, though said to be quite inconclusive, have
too much the appearance of human reason, I have not thought
proper to mention him as a person who has much benefited our
cause; and especially as I understand that "implicit faith"
forms no part of the creed of the above sect.

THE END.

Milton Keynes UK
Ingram Content Group UK Ltd.
UKHW041909120324
439302UK00005B/415